TRAVERSE THEATRE

Over the last three decades Edinburgh's Traverse Theatre has had a seminal influence on British and international theatre. With quality, award-winning productions and programming, the Traverse receives accolades at home and abroad from audiences and critics alike.

Traverse productions have been seen world-wide. Most recently, WIDOWS toured the UK and BONDAGERS toured the world, delighting audiences in London, Toronto and Budapest. After sell-out Edinburgh runs MOSCOW STATIONS transferred to both the West End and New York; UNIDENTIFIED HUMAN REMAINS transferred to London's Hampstead Theatre; and after touring the Highlands and Islands of Scotland KNIVES IN HENS transferred to a sell-out season at the Bush Theatre in London. No stranger to awards, the Traverse recently won the *Scotland on Sunday Critics' Award* for SHINING SOULS by Chris Hannan.

As Scotland's new writing theatre, the Traverse is a powerhouse of quality experimentation, artistic diversity and the place to see the most important contemporary theatre work. The Theatre commissions the best new writers from Scotland and around the world; facilitates numerous script development workshops, rehearsed readings and public writing workshops; and aims to produce six major new theatre productions plus a Scottish touring production each year.

An essential element of the Traverse Company's activities takes place within the educational sector, concentrating on the process of new writing in schools. The Traverse is unique in its exclusive dedication to new writing, providing the infrastructure, professional support and expertise to ensure the development of a sustainable and relevant theatre culture for Scotland and the UK.

BIOGRAPHIES

IONA CARBARNS (*Lynne*): Trained: RSAMD. Theatre work includes: THE MAIDEN STONE, SLEEPING BEAUTY (Royal Lyceum); TARTUFFE, HAVING A BALL (Perth Rep.) and Theatre Workshop's touring Christmas show. Film includes: WHEELS (Barony Films).

VICKY FEATHERSTONE (Director) Trained: Manchester University, and West Yorkshire Playhouse on the Regional Theatre Young Director Scheme. ANNA WEISS is Vicky's first production for the Traverse. Theatre includes: KVETCH, BRIGHTON ROCK (West Yorkshire Playhouse), TWO LIPS INDIFFERENT RED (Bush Theatre), THE GLASS MENAGERIE, A CHRISTMAS CAROL, MY MOTHER SAID I NEVER SHOULD (Bolton Octagon), WOMEN PREFER... (Northern Stage). Other work includes: Script Development Executive for United Film and Television Productions, creating WHERE THE HEART IS and developing TOUCHING EVIL. Vicky has recently been appointed Artistic Director of Paines Plough and her first production, CRAZYHORSE, will tour to the Traverse in October.

JOHN HARRIS (Composer): For the Traverse: SHARP SHORTS. Other theatre work includes: STOCKAREE, OF NETTLES AND ROSES (Theatre Workshop); NOT FOR THE FANFARE (First Base); THE NEST, M'LADY MALADE, THE GREAT THEATRE OF THE WORLD, MANKIND, THE TEMPEST (True Belleek); THE ELVES AND THE SHOEMAKER (Reppe). Musical Direction includes: MASS (Bernstein); AFRICAN SANCTUS (Fanshawe); CARMINA BURANA (Orff); HIAWATHA (Bogdanov). John is also commissioned as a classical composer and works as assistant organist at St Giles' Cathedral, Edinburgh.

TRAVERSE
THEATRE

TRAVERSE THEATRE COMPANY

presents

ANNA WEISS

by Mike Cullen

Lynne	Iona Carbarns
David	John Stahl
Anna	Anne Marie Timoney

Director	Vicky Featherstone
Designer	Mark Leese
Lighting Designer	Chahine Yavroyan
Stage Manager	Gavin Johnston
Deputy Stage Manager	Kay Courteney-Chrystal
Assistant Stage Manager	Victoria Paulo
Wardrobe Supervisor	Lynn Ferguson
Wardrobe Assistant	Alice Taylor
Wardrobe Assistant	Vicki McColl

First performed at the Traverse Theatre
Friday 18 July 1997.

MIKE CULLEN

Since leaving Ross High School in Tranent in 1975, Mike has had a varied working career, including Colliery Electrician, Hospital Porter, Singer/guitarist, and Linguistics Analyst. Since graduating as a mature student from Edinburgh University, with an honours degree in Linguistics, in 1992, Mike has written two successful stage plays - THE CUT, which was produced by Wiseguise Productions and toured Scotland in 1993, transferring to a sell-out run at the Bush Theatre, London, in 1994, and THE COLLECTION, produced by the Traverse Theatre, Edinburgh, in 1995. Both plays were runners up for the George Devine Award, THE CUT was also runner up for the Meyer Whitworth Award. Television work includes STONE COLD, a film for BBC Scene, and MCCALLUM for STV. Work in progress includes the feature film adaptation of THE CUT for Temple Films/BBC Scotland, and a new stage play for the Royal Court Theatre, London. Television work in progress includes the second series of MCCALLUM, the television adaptation of C.S.Forester's HORNBLOWER for United Films/Palace Pictures, and TOUCHING EVIL for United Film and Television, all to be screened in 1998.

MARK LEESE (Designer): For the Traverse: WIDOWS, FAITH HEALER, THE HOPE SLIDE, BROTHERS OF THUNDER, KNIVES IN HENS (also Bush Theatre and Festival '97 production). Other theatre work includes: PARALLEL LINES (Theatre Cryptic); FROGS (Royal National Theatre); BRILLIANT TRACES (Diva/Tron); BABES IN THE WOOD, SNOW WHITE, LOVE & LIBERTY (Tron); BORN GUILTY, THE WAR IN HEAVEN, THE GRAPES OF WRATH, THE SALT WOUND, ANTIGONE (7:84); ON GOLDEN POND (Royal Lyceum); BLACK COMEDY, PUBLIC EYE (Watford Palace). Film includes: CALIFORNIA SUNSHINE (Sigma Films); GOOD DAY FOR THE BAD GUYS (Greenbridge Films); WHAT ELEPHANTS (WWF); CANDY FLOSS (BBC Tartan Short); RUBY (STV First Reels). Mark is currently Design Associate at the Traverse.

JOHN STAHL (David): Trained: RSAMD. For the Traverse: THE ARCHITECT, SHINING SOULS. Other theatre work includes: THE BATTLE OF BAREFOOT (Theatre Space); NEXT TIME I'LL SING TO YOU, THE GAME (Edinburgh Festival); ALADDIN, THE CARETAKER, WHAT THE BUTLER SAW, THE GLASS MENAGERIE, ZOO STORY, ENTERTAINING MR SLOANE (Cumbernauld); THE SASH and THE GAME (Glasgow Pavilion); LENT (Lyric); BENEATH ONE BANNER (7:84); COMMEDIA (Sheffield Crucible/Lyric/King's, Edinburgh); MACBETH, THE SLEEPING BEAUTY, PADDY'S MARKET, THE REAL WURLD? (Tron); DEATH OF A SALESMAN, THE SNOW QUEEN, THE CRUCIBLE (Royal Lyceum); ALADDIN (Adam Smith); HAMLET, COMEDIANS (Belgrade, Coventry); CINDERELLA (Dundee Rep). Television includes: YOU'RE A GOOD BOY, SON, A SENSE OF FREEDOM, CAMERON ON CAMERA, GARNOCK WAY, HIGH ROAD, ALBERT AND THE LION, CRIME STORY, TAGGART (STV); THE McKINNONS, RESORT TO MURDER, PARAHANDY, DR FINLAY (BBC). Film work includes LOCH NESS.

ANNE MARIE TIMONEY (*Anna*): Trained: RSAMD. Fot the Traverse: WORMWOOD, WIDOWS, STONES AND ASHES. Other theatre work includes: ASYLUM, ASYLUM, HUGHIE ON THE WIRES (Wiseguise); ONE, TWO, HEY (Arches & touring); HUGHIE ON THE WIRES (Calypso, Dublin); PRE PARADISE SORRY NOW, THE HOUSEKEEPER, ANTHONY, WITTGENSTEIN'S DAUGHTER (Citizens'); CONQUEST OF THE SOUTH POLE, ONE FLEW OVER THE CUCKOO'S NEST (Rain Dog); THE WICKED LADIES (Old Athenaeum, Women 2000); MARLENE - FALLING IN LOVE AGAIN (A.B.C. Theatre Co.); OTHELLO, DEATH OF A SALESMAN, THE MERCHANT OF VENICE (Royal Lyceum); ROAD, LONG STORY SHORT (7:84). Television includes: TAGGART, CRIME FILE, HIGH ROAD, DR FINLAY (STV); THE LONG ROADS, RAB C. NESBITT, RUFFIAN HEARTS, EX-S, BAD BOYS, ATHLETICO PARTICK (BBC). Radio includes: STAND UP NORMA JEAN (BBC). Film work includes: CARLA'S SONG, RIFF RAFF, A CHILL, WILD FLOWERS, SNAKE WOMAN, KARMIC MOTHERS (BBC Tartan Short).

CHAHINE YAVROYAN (Lighting Designer): Trained: Bristol Old Vic Theatre School. For the Traverse: THE ARCHITECT, SHINING SOULS. Other theatre work includes: THE TRIAL, METAMORPHOSIS, MISS JULIE, ZOO STORY, AGAMEMNON (Stephen Berkoff); PEOPLE SHOWS NO.84 to NO.101... and counting; MACBETH (Leicester Haymarket); USES OF ENCHANTMENT (ICA); THE LITTLE BLACK BOOK (French Institute); ENNIO MARCHETTO (Hackney Empire); LA MUSICA DEUXIEME, GAUCHO (Hampstead); HEDDA GABLER, WOLK'S WORLD (Manchester Royal Exchange); PYGMALION (Nottingham Playhouse); DARWIN'S FLOOD (Bush); TANTAMOUNT ESPERANCE (Royal Court); HAMLET (Kaboodle). Dance work includes: 15 MINUTES TO 6 HOURS (Anatomy Dance Theatre); GLORIA, I SURRENDER DEAR (The Place); HAUGHMOND DANCES (Haughmond Abbey); ASCENDING FIELDS (Fort Dunlop); FOREST DANCES (Purcell Room). Site specific work includes: HOUSE (Station House Opera, Salisbury) and various events and celebrations for the city of Bologna, Italy.

**ANNA WEISS props, costumes & scenery
built by Traverse workshops.**
Funded by the National Lottery

**For generous help with ANNA WEISS
the Traverse Theatre thanks:**

Scenic Artist: Ursula Cleary;
Production Placements: Laura Cockroft,
Emily Munro, Jennifer Stroud
Administration Placement: Justin McLean

H. Karnac (Books) Limited, 58 Gloucester Road,
London, SW7 4QY,
tel 0171 584 3303, fax 0171 823 7743.
John Wiley's & Sons Ltd, Sage Publications,
BLF, HarperCollins Publishers, Dr Susan Ramsay,
Macro,
John Ritchie & Sons (clockmakers), Phone-in,
Royal Lyceum Theatre Company, Bert Braithwell.

LEVER BROTHERS for Wardrobe Care.
Print Photography by Euan Myles.
Production Photography by Kevin Low.

TRAVERSE THEATRE • SPONSORSHIP

Sponsorship income enables the Traverse to commission and produce new plays and offer audiences a diverse and exciting programme of events throughout the year.

We would like to thank the following companies for their support throughout the year.

CORPORATE ASSOCIATE SCHEME

LEVEL ONE
Dundas & Wilson CS
Scottish Brewers
Scottish Life Assurance Co
United Distillers

LEVEL TWO
Allingham & Co, Solicitors
Isle of Skye 8 Year Blend
Laurence Smith - Wine Merchants
NB Information
Mactaggart and Mickel Ltd
Métier Recruitment
Willis Corroon Scotland Ltd

LEVEL THREE
Alistir Tait FGA Antique & Fine Jewellery, Gerrard & Medd, Designers, KPMG, Moores Rowland Chartered Accountants, Nicholas Groves Raines Architects, Scottish Post Office Board

With thanks to:
Navy Blue Design, designers for the Traverse
and to George Stewarts the printers.
Robin Arnott of the Royal Bank of Scotland for his advise on information technology and systems.
This placement was arranged through Business In The Arts.

The Traverse Theatre's work would not be possible without the support of:

The Traverse receives financial assistance for its educational and development work from:
Calouste Gulbenkian Foundation,
Esmee Fairbairn Charitable Trust,
The Peggy Ramsay Foundation,
The Nancie Massey Charitable Trust
Scottish International Education Trust
Charity No.SC 002368

TRAVERSE THEATRE • THE COMPANY

Claire Beattie
Education Co-ordinator

Maria Bechaalani
Asst Electrician

Stephen Bremner
Asst Bar Manager

Vian Curtis
Production Technician

Kay Courteney-Chrystal
Deputy Stage Manager

Emma Dall
Finance Assistant

Rachel Davidson
Deputy Bar Manager

Lynn Ferguson
Wardrobe Supervisor

Tim Follett
Deputy Electrician

Sarah Gardiner
Administrative Support

Mike Griffiths
Production Manager

Paul Hackett
Finance Manager

Noelle Henderson
Development Manager

Philip Howard
Artistic Director

Louise Ironside
Associate Playwright

Ruth Kent
Asst Box Office Mgr

Gavin Johnston
Stage Manager

Mark Leese
Design Associate

Niall Macdonald
Bar Manager

Jude MacLaverty
Marketing/Box Office Asst

Jan McTaggart
Marketing & Press Officer

Jenny Mainland
Administrative Asst

Colin Marr
Theatre/Commercial Manager

Lucy Mason
Administrative Producer

Alex Musgrave
Box Office Manager

Lorraine May
Front of House Mgr

Victoria Paulo
Asst Stage Manager

Renny Robertson
Chief Electrician

Hannah Rye
Literary Assistant

Kirstie Skinner
Assistant Administrator

Fiona Sturgeon
Marketing Manager

John Tiffany
Literary Director

Ella Wildridge
Literary Associate

TRAVERSE THEATRE - BOARD OF DIRECTORS

Tom Mitchell, President, **John Scott Moncrieff**, Chair,
Harry McCann, Vice Chair, **Scott Howard**, Secretary,
**Barry Ayre, Paul Chima, Stuart Hepburn,
Sir Eddie Kulukundis, Muriel Murray**

*This play is dedicated to Nick Marston, my agent,
for his endless enthusiasm and faith, and to
Peter Arnott, for giving me the right directions.*

Mike Cullen, July 1997

ANNA WEISS

I thought I saw, upon the stair
A little man who wasn't there
He wasn't there again today
Oh, how I wish he'd go away

Children's rhyme

Characters

ANNA – late thirties, a private hypnotherapist

DAVID – early forties

LYNN – David's daughter, early twenties

The action takes place in Anna's flat

ACT ONE – the eve of moving out

ACT TWO – later the same evening

The actors should feel free to use their own, natural,
uninflected accent, regardless of the production location.

Act One

The living room of ANNA WEISS's *flat. The flat is almost empty, save for a number of large tea chests, which are packed with possessions, and a couple of old wooden chairs. There are two exits, one to the street, the other to the rest of the flat. Four suitcases sit near the street exit.*

Enter LYNN, *jeans and a T-Shirt. She crosses to the first chest, starts to rummage through it. Enter* ANNA, *smartly dressed, carrying some books, which she places in another of the chests. She talks at breakneck speed.*

ANNA. And just in case you're interested, I hadn't finished.

LYNN. What?

ANNA. Talking, I hadn't finished talking.

LYNN. Sorry.

ANNA. I turn around, you've wandered off again, I'm talking to myself.

LYNN. I'm sorry.

ANNA. Which is fine. (*Pause.*) Only I don't need to hear it.

ANNA *exits into the flat.*

LYNN (*looking over her shoulder*). I said I was . . .

LYNN *sighs, resumes her search. Enter* ANNA, *carrying more books, which she places in the chest.*

ANNA. And while I might be the first to admit that I like the sound of my own voice, I generally don't indulge in conversation without a purpose, without some *point* which I think may or may not be of *use* to you.

LYNN. I said I was sorry.

ANNA. I mean far be it from me to decide what you should or shouldn't listen to, I'm only the one with experience.

ANNA *exits again.*

ANNA (*Offstage, raising her voice*). Ten years of experience, to be exact, dealing, solving, *healing* case after case exactly like yours, experience which, judging by your lack of interest, you seem on a mission to ignore.

ANNA *returns carrying three wine glasses, which she places on the floor.*

ANNA. Not that I want you to feel compelled to listen to whatever *garbage* I no doubt continually spew *forth*, but . . .

LYNN. I thought you'd finished.

ANNA. . . . every day, hearing myself, endlessly repeating stuff, stuff, I might add, which is drawn from that well of ten years experience, however useless that might be.

Pause.

LYNN. I thought you'd finished.

Pause.

ANNA. Which means what?

Pause.

LYNN. . . . which means . . . ?

ANNA. Which means you weren't listening.

LYNN. I *was* listening, I thought you'd finished.

Pause.

ANNA. So, where did I get to?

LYNN. Where do you always get to?

ANNA. No, you said you were listening, and if that's true, then you'll know what I said.

Pause.

So?

LYNN. What?

ANNA. What did I say?

   Pause.

LYNN. I don't know . . .

ANNA. Hah!

LYNN. . . . but it was probably something impressively clever.

ANNA. I knew it.

LYNN. You're right . . .

ANNA. I knew you weren't . . .

LYNN. I wasn't listening, you win. (*Pause.*) Carry on.

   Pause.

ANNA. Doesn't matter.

LYNN. I'm listening now.

ANNA. I've forgotten it now.

LYNN. You've forgotten it?

ANNA. Probably wasn't worth hearing anyway.

LYNN. Fair enough.

ANNA. Just me rambling away . . .

LYNN. That's fair enough.

ANNA. . . . getting to where I always get to. Apparently.

   She exits again, returns a few moments later with two
   bottles of wine, red and white, which she proceeds to
   uncork.

ANNA (*as she enters*). What I was saying, and I know you
   don't want to hear it, and it's probably lost all *impact* by
   now, and the last thing I want is to is to . . . you know what
   I think about people who *generalise*, but all men, and I
   mean *all* men, share a common affliction . . . somebody
   should write a book . . . in fact, *I'll* write it, and you know
   what I'll call it? Hole Blindness – The Male Affliction.

Because, and stop me if I'm wrong, but a man, any man, looks at a woman, any woman, what does he see? A hole to be filled. And that's it. And it doesn't matter what age the woman is, the old woman in the post office queue, drawing her pension – *used* to be a hole to be filled, the young girl on the baby swing at the park – will *be* a hole to be filled, you go walking down the street with your skirt hitched up and your legs wide open, that, sweetheart, is a man. (*Pause.*) And if there's one thing I've learned, it's this – desire knows no boundaries. Class, race, sex, *age*, all invisible to your average male on a hole hunt. (*Pause.*) Sad thing is, they don't even realise it, they, they what? Disguise, dress it up, romance, marriage, fancy underpants. (*Pause.*) The Love of a Caring Father, anything to make it look attractive, and believe me, they're good at it, they know just the right buttons to press, convince you that you're something more, but the bottom line, when everything's stripped away, you're a big pink gaping hole that must be filled.

Pause.

I mean, God knows, and I hope you're listening, I hope you're *hearing* this, but I been through that, a million times, men, queuing down the street, bearing gifts, flies undone.

Pause.

But there comes a time when you you you wake up, I don't mean from sleep, you're not even asleep, but you wake up, from from what you've *been*.

Pause.

You think, you think, is this what I am? This this this . . . hole? You're wandering around like the walking dead, I know how that feels, believe me, but let me tell you, Lynn, you listening? Let me tell you, choosing *life*, choosing to *live*, that's the hardest thing.

LYNN. I take it there's a point to all of this.

Pause.

ANNA. A point? Of course there's a point.

Pause.

LYNN. So, tell me.

ANNA. What?

LYNN. The point.

ANNA. The point?

LYNN. You said there was a . . .

ANNA. The point is, the point is I shouldn't even have to explain what the point is.

LYNN. There isn't one, is there?

ANNA. You should *know* what the point is.

LYNN. You just open your mouth . . .

ANNA. By now, you should know.

LYNN. You just open your mouth . . .

ANNA. Okay, okay, you want a point? Here's a point . . . how much do you really know? (*Pause.*) About men, about the nature of men, their desires, what scares them . . .

LYNN. Why would I want . . .

ANNA. You need to know, be *sure*, be *certain*, and I know what I'm talking about, here, the way they *work*, the tacky *tricks*, your only defence? *Know* what scares them. *Know* what scares them, and you got them round the throat. What scares them? The same, the very same thing that they desire, which is? Lynn?

Pause. LYNN *is searching through the box again.*

The hole. The hole. Terrifies the living . . . it's where they came from, and where they spend their entire bloody lives trying to get back to, scares the living death out of them, does he like red or white?

Pause.

Lynn?

LYNN. What?

ANNA. Does he like . . . (*Pause.*) You did it again.

LYNN. What?

ANNA. I don't believe . . .

LYNN. What?

ANNA. Just now.

LYNN. What did I do?

ANNA. You stopped listening.

Pause.

LYNN. Just because I'm not talking doesn't mean I'm not listening. (*Pause.*) In fact, I seem to remember that not talking is kind of an essential *part* of listening.

Pause.

ANNA. I asked you a question.

LYNN. I know.

ANNA. What was it?

Pause.

LYNN. You want me to repeat the question?

ANNA. What did I . . .

LYNN. You want me to . . .

ANNA. What did I say?

LYNN. What is this, some kind of test?

ANNA. What was the question?

Pause.

LYNN. Oh, I know what this is.

ANNA. You weren't list . . .

LYNN. This is tonight, isn't it?

Pause.

ANNA. . . . tonight . . . ?

LYNN. This is . . . just because I didn't consult you . . .

Pause.

ANNA. Consult me? Why would you need to . . .

LYNN. Just because I didn't . . .

ANNA. I mean, for God's sake, Lynn . . .

LYNN. But this . . .

ANNA. Consult me?

LYNN. This . . .

ANNA. What does that say about me?

LYNN. It's something I had to . . .

ANNA. What does that make me?

LYNN. Now *you're* the one that's not . . .

ANNA. What the hell do I know anyway?

Pause. ANNA *pours herself a drink.*

ANNA. Would you like one of these?

LYNN. What?

ANNA. A drink, would you like a . . . Would. You. Like.
A. Drink?

Pause.

LYNN. Yes, thank you, I would.

Pause.

ANNA. Red or white?

LYNN. Doesn't matter.

ANNA. You have a choice. There's red, and on the other hand,
there's white.

LYNN. Whatever.

ANNA. Be a devil, make a choice.

LYNN. I don't care.

ANNA. I know you like red.

LYNN. I'll have red.

ANNA. But it's always good to have a change.

LYNN. Okay, I'll have white, then.

Pause.

ANNA. You hate white.

LYNN. So, why did you ask me?

ANNA. It was your decision.

Pause.

LYNN. Whatever has the most alcohol.

ANNA. The red.

LYNN. Fine.

ANNA pours another glass, carries it across to LYNN, who takes it, takes a sip, puts down the glass, then resumes her search of the box.

Pause.

ANNA. Shouldn't you be getting ready?

LYNN. Ready?

Pause.

ANNA. You intend to meet him looking like that?

LYNN. Like what?

ANNA. Dirty jeans and T-shirt with stain, what does that say?

LYNN. What does it . . .

ANNA. What does that tell him?

LYNN. What does it matter what I look like?

ANNA. It matters, young lady, it matters because . . . 'you feel how you look'. Who said that? (*Pause.*) Probably me, you feel how you look, which means we each of us, we can influence how we feel, by choosing how we look, is that clever? I don't know.

LYNN. Well, this must be how I feel, then.

Pause.

ANNA. Dirty Jeans and T-Shirt with Stain, you feel Dirty Jeans and T-Shirt with Stain?

LYNN. No, I feel like shit. This is a compromise.

LYNN *knocks back the rest of her wine.*

ANNA. And you're drinking too fast.

LYNN. Just 'influencing how I feel'.

Pause. LYNN *resumes her search.*

ANNA. So, is this a personal obsession, or can anyone join in?

LYNN. What?

ANNA. The Search for the Holy Grail.

Pause.

LYNN. I put it in here.

Pause.

ANNA (*the thing*). What?

LYNN. I remember doing it.

Pause.

ANNA. Good. (*Pause.*) It'll still be there, then.

LYNN. What?

ANNA. The thing you lost.

LYNN. It isn't lost.

ANNA. No?

LYNN. It's here.

ANNA. Right.

LYNN. This is where I put it, this is where it'll be.

ANNA. Good.

Long pause.

ANNA. You found it?

LYNN. Not yet.

ANNA. But it's not lost.

LYNN. Nope.

Pause.

ANNA. When does a thing become lost?

LYNN. What?

ANNA. At what point will you call it lost?

LYNN. I don't know.

ANNA. Because there has to be a point, when you're looking for something, and you can't find it, a point when you say, 'Well, that's it lost, then'.

LYNN. It isn't lost.

ANNA. Not yet.

LYNN. No.

ANNA. But it will be soon.

LYNN. I'll find it before then.

ANNA. Before it's officially lost.

LYNN. Yeah.

Pause.

ANNA *hovers, her presence eventually getting to* LYNN.

LYNN. Look, Anna, tonight is something I have to . . .

ANNA. It's okay.

LYNN. Tonight is *my* decision . . .

ANNA. I under . . .

LYNN. . . . by *me*, without any . . .

ANNA. It's really okay.

Pause.

I mean, why should I care, why should I, really?

Pause.

Year and a half bloody *purgatory*, getting you, pushing you through it, why should I, what the . . .

LYNN. Pushing . . . ?

ANNA. . . . what the hell do I know?

Pause.

LYNN. What do you mean pushing?

ANNA. Other than the fact that, for some reason which is way beyond any scope of understanding, you couldn't find it in yourself to *come* to me with this.

LYNN. I've explained, no, wait, why should I even *have* to ex . . .

ANNA. Of course, I should have foreseen this, after what you've been through, it's completely understandable you should develop this preoccupation with self . . .

LYNN. Now just hang on . . .

ANNA. . . . but I don't think it's an unfair expectation that that the part I've played, however useless, in your recovery, your *dis*covery, should bring with it certain certain entitlements . . .

LYNN. You're making . . .

ANNA. . . . certain basic human entitlements, such as respect . . .

LYNN. . . . you're . . .

ANNA. Or or or or if not respect, you could have at the very least have maybe *patronised* me by mentioning the thing in passing.

LYNN. Okay, I'm sorry, right? I'm sorry I didn't mention it, I'm sorry I didn't ask your permission.

Pause.

ANNA. So this is it, is it? This is what I'm to have? Year and a half of my *life*?

LYNN. No. I'm . . . I didn't intend for you to feel . . .

ANNA. Year and a half of sacrifices . . .

LYNN. Look. For this to *work*, it has to come from *me*, without any help, I have to . . .

ANNA. . . . every waking moment, living with it . . .

LYNN. Anna . . .

ANNA. . . . suffering . . .

LYNN. Oh, piss off!

Pause. LYNN *resumes her search.*

ANNA. It may seem, and I don't blame you for this, but in the way that I behave, in the face I *present*, it may seem that I have a pretty tough hide. But sometimes, just sometimes . . .

LYNN. *You* gave me the book.

Pause.

ANNA. What book?

LYNN. The book which . . .

ANNA. I gave you lots of *books* . . .

LYNN. The one about survival.

Pause.

ANNA. And this is what this is?

LYNN. You gave me the book, I *read* the book . . .

ANNA. We're talking about a book?

LYNN. Have you read it?

ANNA. Is this what we're talking about?

LYNN. Have you read it?

Pause.

ANNA. Of course I've . . .

LYNN. The chapter on confrontation, you read that?

Pause.

ANNA. Books are one thing . . .

LYNN. I read the book, I know what to do.

ANNA. Books are, well they're useful, but . . .

LYNN. I know what to do, Anna.

Pause.

ANNA. Because it's in a book?

LYNN. You don't understand.

ANNA. No, I understand completely, you read it in a *book*,
    looks like an easy *thing*, you think you're *ready* . . .

LYNN. I just can't up and *leave* without . . .

ANNA. Well, you think you're ready, you go right ahead.

LYNN. You don't think I'm ready?

Pause.

ANNA. That's not for me to say, is it? (*Pause.*) And even if I
    did choose to voice an opinion, chances are, you wouldn't
    hear it anyway, because it seems I've developed this
    remarkable ability to think I'm talking when I'm not.

LYNN. I give up.

ANNA. Fine.

Pause.

LYNN. And just for the record, you asked me if my father
    liked red wine or white, and the answer is, I don't
    remember, and even if I did, I don't actually *give* a fuck,
    and I don't even know why you're opening wine the fucking
    first place.

Pause.

ANNA. It's traditional.

LYNN. Traditional?

ANNA. Last night in a house, you you drink, to what's been, to what's to come.

LYNN. Oh right, the old 'Moving House *Drinking* Tradition'.

Pause.

ANNA. Can't stand them, myself.

LYNN. What?

ANNA. Last nights. Bloody depressing. (*Pause.*) Stuck in limbo, neither one place nor the other, not quite gone, not quite arrived. (*Pause.*) Last time I moved, the last night, I booked into a hotel. (*Pause.*) Lay awake all night feeling sorry for myself. (*Pause.*) But they do that to you, hotels, no-one to talk to, too much time to think. (*Pause.*) Much better, don't you think, to make a clean break, get out before the end, no regrets. (*Pause.*) Make the decision and just go. (*Pause.*) Because you get obsessed, with tidying up, with everything put in its *place*, the old life neatly *resolved*, you you you feel *obliged*, say *goodbyes*, all that *crap*, what you *don't* see, what you *don't* see – that it's already resolved for *you*, it became resolved the minute the decision was made, the second you decided to move on, it was resolved for *you*, and these feelings of of of *completion*, the need to complete rests with *others*, and they tug on you like a nagging doubt, but true, *true* liberation lies in having the courage to *avoid* such endings, being brave enough to walk away. (*Pause.*) Like tonight, you feel obliged to stay, to tidy up, but there's no *need*, you see? Do you see? And that's my advice, for what it's worth, we get in the car, we get in the car and go, just go, right now, up and leave this life for *others* to resolve. (*Pause.*) What do you say?

LYNN. Why don't you go?

ANNA. What?

LYNN. You go on ahead.

ANNA. On my own?

LYNN. I'll come later.

Pause.

ANNA. You want me to go?

LYNN. I can get the train.

ANNA. I don't understand.

Pause.

LYNN. It's quite simple, you drive to the new house tonight, I'll get the train in the morning.

ANNA. Why would you want to do that?

LYNN. I don't.

Pause.

ANNA. So why would you even suggest . . .

LYNN. You're the one going on about it.

Pause.

ANNA. We chose the house together.

LYNN. So?

ANNA. So, we'll arrive together.

LYNN. I really don't mind.

ANNA. I do. (*Pause.*) I mean I was under the impression, and maybe I'm wrong, but I thought that was the whole *point*. (*Pause.*) To to to set *out*. (*Pause.*) A new *start*, all *that* . . .

LYNN. Fine.

ANNA. The the the defining moment . . .

LYNN. We'll go . . .

ANNA. The new frontier . . .

LYNN. We'll go tomorrow.

Pause.

ANNA. Not just straggling along . . .

LYNN. I said we'll . . .

ANNA. . . . turning up when it suits.

LYNN. I can't leave before I see him.

Pause.

ANNA. Well, I'm obviously not making myself clear enough, here, and and . . . maybe I am, maybe you just don't want to hear it, but . . .

LYNN. I've made up my . . .

ANNA. Could you, could you do me one favour, please? As a friend. Could you please just listen for one . . .

LYNN. There's no . . .

ANNA. . . . one tiny fucking minute! (*Pause.*) Do you think you owe me that?

Pause.

And now look. (*Pause.*) What we come to, calling in favours like children, you see? You see what this does to us?

LYNN. 'Us'?

ANNA. You see what this . . .

LYNN. This has nothing to *do* with . . .

ANNA. After all that we've been through, all we've *achieved* together, you want to risk all that for some stupid thing you read in a . . .

LYNN. It isn't stupid . . .

ANNA. Well, what is it? What? Explain it to me.

Pause.

LYNN. It's . . .

ANNA. It's the memories.

LYNN. No, it's . . .

ANNA. You're having doubts.

LYNN. No.

ANNA. You're thinking, 'maybe I'm wrong, maybe none of these things happened' . . .

LYNN. I'm not . . .

ANNA. . . . maybe if I confront him, look into his eyes, he'll give himself away, and then I'll know'.

LYNN. That's not . . .

ANNA. 'Then I'll know for sure.'

LYNN. I don't *have* any doubts. (*Pause.*) I don't need . . .

ANNA. And all the time, all the time, he'll be sitting there, rubbing his hands.

LYNN. These things happened, I know that they . . .

ANNA. Rubbing his hands, and laughing inside . . .

LYNN. I don't need confirmation.

ANNA. . . . laughing inside like they always do, with that look on his face . . .

LYNN. I need . . .

ANNA. . . . that says, that says, 'I'm not listening, cos you're just a hole, and holes can't talk, so don't even try'.

Pause.

LYNN. I need to let him know how I feel! (*Pause.*) It's my *right*. (*Pause.*) All those *years*, he should *know*, he should *know*, how much I *hate* him, I want to look into his eyes, and see he *understands*, and see how much it *hurts*.

Pause.

ANNA. And you think that's what you'll get?

LYNN. I don't know, I have to . . .

ANNA. You think he'll feel any kind of remorse? (*Pause.*) All you're doing, all you're doing, you're making it easier for *him*, you see? You're making it easier for him by letting him think that *you* have a problem with it. Do you see?

LYNN. I don't have a problem with it.

ANNA. I know that. But he doesn't, he thinks you *do*, by even *talking* to him . . .

LYNN. I have to do this, Anna.

Pause.

ANNA. Lynn Lynn Lynn Lynn Lynn. Listen to me. Lynn. You listening? (*Pause.*) You believe in what you're doing, I can see that, but trust me on this, it's the wrong thing, it's exactly the wrong thing.

LYNN. I don't think it is.

ANNA. I mean, what I'm . . . what has led you to this this *certainty* can often be, well it can often be the need for *comfort*, and comfort can always be found in the status quo.

Pause.

LYNN. I don't understand.

ANNA. Can I ask you something? The last few months, have we been happy?

LYNN. What?

ANNA. Have we been happy, it's a simple . . .

LYNN. You know we've been . . .

ANNA. Last few months, we've felt happy, more, yeah?

LYNN (*wary*). I don't understand.

Pause.

ANNA. To be happy, in your case, is to know that it must end in pain. Every time you've ever been happy in your life, that's what happens, the incidents you recalled, most of them, you'll find, were preceded by happiness. (*Pause.*) You're in bed, comfortable, happy, and bang, you're . . . he buys you something nice, maybe an ice-cream, maybe a new dress, and bang, in your head, the pay off for being

happy is always pain. (*Pause.*) It's what you fear, what you
expect, you you might even go looking for it.

LYNN. Go looking for it?

ANNA. Go searching for the thing that hurts you.

Pause.

LYNN. I want to be hurt?

ANNA. That's right. (*Pause.*) Because you expect it,
sometimes, and I know this sounds . . . but sometimes, you
even need it, to feel that pain, to feel worthless again, it
makes sense to you, so you seek it out.

Pause.

LYNN. Why would I want to feel worthless?

ANNA. Because it's what you've always been. (*Pause.*)
Because that's what he made you. (*Pause.*) But understand
this, I respect you. Please hear that. (*Pause.*) I respect what
you're doing, the courage you're showing, I don't think I've
ever respected anyone more in my life, it's just . . .

Pause.

LYNN. What?

ANNA. If it feels right for you, then who am I to say . . .

LYNN. What is it?

ANNA. It's a question of strength.

Pause.

LYNN. I feel strong enough to . . .

ANNA. No, it's not that simple. It's . . . what you discovered
. . . you think you're strong in what you know, but . . .

LYNN. I have my list, I feel strong enough to . . .

ANNA. List, what list?

Pause.

LYNN. Like it says in the book.

ANNA. Forget the book, what list?

LYNN. The things he did. I wrote them down, like it said in the book . . .

ANNA. Will you forget the bloody book just for one . . .

LYNN. I wrote them down, so that nothing gets forgotten when I read them out.

Long pause.

ANNA. He won't listen.

LYNN. He'll have no . . .

ANNA. He won't hear a single word.

LYNN. I'll make him . . .

ANNA. Believe me, Lynn, I've seen this, so many times I've . . . all he wants, all he wants is one tiny weakness, one thing he can use . . .

LYNN. Why do you have such a problem with this?

Pause.

ANNA. Me?

LYNN. I mean, I thought you'd be pleased, that I took it on myself, to *decide*, like you keep saying, make *decisions* . . .

ANNA. This is different . . .

LYNN. Take *control*, you said . . .

ANNA. This is this is . . .

LYNN. That's what I'm doing, taking control.

ANNA. No, you're . . .

LYNN. I don't see why you would have a problem with that.

ANNA. Look at yourself, Lynn. (*Pause.*) Just stop for a moment and look at what you're doing.

Pause.

LYNN. What?

ANNA. This thing, that you've lost . . .

LYNN. It isn't lost.

ANNA. Misplaced, then. Don't you see? This is the fourth
time this week you've lost something or other, you think
that's down to chance?

LYNN. What're you . . .

ANNA. Look at it, Lynn. Look and see. Four times in one
week, you're all over the house, always searching, hours on
end, looking for something or other.

Pause.

LYNN. We're moving house.

ANNA. No . . .

LYNN. Everything's a mess . . .

ANNA. No, don't *do* this to yourself, don't mess yourself up
with *pretence* and *excuse*, it's a *symbol*, you *know* it, it's all
the same thing.

Pause.

LYNN. I don't understand.

ANNA. It's what scares you.

LYNN. Wait, wait, just go back a . . .

ANNA. What scares you? Discovery, finding the answers,
confirmation, that it *happened*, that you're *right*, that the
memories are *real*, it's all the same thing, and it's a
terrifying prospect, much easier to just keep looking, much
easier never to find anything. You see?

Pause.

LYNN. You're saying I, what, that I've deliberately lost . . .

ANNA. I'm saying you're scared, of tonight, of him, of the
truth, and even if it's there, even if his eyes give him away,
you won't see it, you won't see it, because you're not ready
to see it.

Pause.

LYNN. I remember putting it in this box.

Pause.

ANNA. You *think* you . . .

LYNN. In detail, I remember in detail. (*Pause.*) . . . approaching this box . . .

ANNA. Lynn . . .

LYNN. . . . putting the thing in the box . . .

ANNA. Lynn . . .

LYNN. I can see myself doing it.

ANNA. Listen to me . . .

LYNN. I can see myself.

ANNA. You're doing it again.

LYNN. What?

ANNA. You're doing it again.

LYNN. Doing what?

ANNA. Getting yourself all wound up over . . .

LYNN. I put it in the box!

Pause.

I put it in the box.

Pause.

ANNA. Okay. (*Pause.*) That's fine. (*Pause.*) I thought we'd be through this.

LYNN. What?

ANNA. I thought, by now, we'd be beyond . . .

LYNN. What are you talking about?

Pause.

ANNA. Have you tried the other boxes?

Pause.

LYNN. There's no need.

Pause.

ANNA. You might at least look.

LYNN. I don't have to. This is the box.

Pause.

ANNA. Maybe you took it out.

LYNN. When?

ANNA. I don't know, I'm just saying . . .

LYNN. Did you see me take it out?

ANNA. . . . maybe you did.

Pause.

LYNN. Did you see me take it out?

Pause.

ANNA. Well, no, but . . .

LYNN. Then why say you did?

ANNA. I didn't say you did, I said maybe you did. Maybe you took it out and put it somewhere else and forgot about it.

Pause.

LYNN. I took it out and forgot about it?

ANNA. Maybe you did.

Pause.

LYNN. I came up to the box, took it out, put it somewhere else, and forgot about it, is that it?

Pause.

ANNA. Look . . .

LYNN. That what you're . . .

ANNA. I don't even know what we're talking about.

LYNN. Great.

Pause.

ANNA. If I knew what it was . . .

LYNN. I just forgot about . . .

ANNA. If I knew what it was, then maybe I could . . .

LYNN. I approached the box, I went inside, rummaged around, found the thing, lifted it, lifted it from the box, carried it somewhere else, placed it in this other place wherever that might be, all of these things, and I just forgot.

ANNA. It happens.

LYNN. Not to me.

Pause.

LYNN (*searching the box again*). Approached, rummaged, found . . . CARRIED! That what you're saying?

ANNA. Every time, you do this every . . .

LYNN. Is that what you're saying?

ANNA. Well maybe *I* moved it, whatever it . . .

LYNN. You?

ANNA. What does it matter?

LYNN. You moved it?

ANNA. Maybe I did.

Pause.

LYNN. Where?

ANNA. This is getting . . .

LYNN. Where did you put it?

ANNA. Well, if I knew that . . .

LYNN. You've forgotten?

ANNA. . . . . I'd maybe know . . .

LYNN. You remember taking it out?

ANNA. . . . know what it is . . .

LYNN. You remember that?

ANNA. . . . I'm supposed to have fucking *moved*.

Pause.

LYNN. Either you do or you don't.

Pause.

ANNA. Okay, okay, I moved it.

LYNN. Now we're getting to it.

ANNA. I took it out of the box . . .

LYNN. Why would you . . .

ANNA. I took it out of the box, put it somewhere else just to get on your nerves.

Pause.

LYNN. Now you're just being stupid.

ANNA. No no, I deliberately hid it somewhere, and then I made a point of forgetting where I put it, just so's you wouldn't find it, and get upset.

LYNN. I hate when you get fucking . . .

ANNA. LOOK . . . in the other . . . fucking . . . BOXES!

Pause. LYNN tips the box over, empties out the contents – possessions everywhere.

ANNA. Jesus Christ.

LYNN. I put it here, it'll still be here.

She rummages through the possessions, picking stuff up, throwing it around.

LYNN. It must be here. (*Pause.*) It must be here.

ANNA (*approaching her*). Lynn.

LYNN. I can see myself doing it.

ANNA. Lynn. Stop this. Lynn.

LYNN. I can see myself.

ANNA. Do you hear me? Lynn? Stop this. Right now. Stop it.

She puts his hand on her shoulder. LYNN *goes rigid.*

LYNN (*screaming*). I see myself!

ANNA. Lynn.

LYNN. I see it!

ANNA. Okay.

LYNN. I see it!

ANNA. It's okay.

LYNN. No!

ANNA *hugs her.*

ANNA. Let it out.

LYNN (*breaking down*). I see it happening.

ANNA. I know.

LYNN. I see myself.

ANNA. Let it go.

LYNN. I see myself.

ANNA. Let it go. (*Pause.*) Just let it go.

Pause.

LYNN. I can see.

ANNA. I know.

LYNN. I know what happened.

ANNA. Just let it go.

LYNN. I can see it.

ANNA. Ssh.

Long pause.

ANNA. Let's look in the other boxes.

LYNN. This was the . . .

ANNA. Ssh.

She kisses her on the top of the head, takes her by the hand, leads her to another box.

ANNA. What is it we're looking for?

Pause.

LYNN. The picture.

ANNA. What picture?

LYNN. The one of me, when I was nine.

Pause.

ANNA. The one with your Dad?

LYNN *nods.*

ANNA. What do you want with it?

LYNN. I want to see it.

ANNA. Why?

LYNN. Because . . .

ANNA. You know it won't do you . . .

LYNN. Because I have to see it.

Pause.

ANNA. Why not wait, until after the . . .

LYNN. I want to see it now! (*Pause.*) I have to see it before I see him again. I haven't seen him in a year, I can barely remember what he looks like. I don't want him turning up, not knowing what he *looks* like.

Pause.

ANNA. Okay, let's see.

She rummages in the box for a second, pulls out a photograph.

ANNA. This it?

Pause. LYNN *stares at the photograph.*

LYNN. I never put it in there.

ANNA. It's okay.

LYNN. I never . . .

ANNA. I must've moved it, okay?

Pause.

LYNN. When?

ANNA. What?

LYNN. When did you move it?

ANNA. I don't know.

LYNN. Why did you move it?

ANNA. I don't know, things get moved, what does it matter, you've got it now.

Pause.

LYNN. You didn't want me to find it.

ANNA. What?

LYNN. That's why you moved it.

ANNA. I don't . . .

LYNN. You knew I would look . . .

ANNA. If I'd wanted to hide it . . .

LYNN. You deliberately . . .

ANNA (*overlapping*). If I'd wanted . . .

LYNN (*overlapping*). . . . put it where you knew I wouldn't look.

Pause.

ANNA. Why would I show you where it was?

End of Act One.

Act Two

The same, a little later. ANNA *and* DAVID *sit on the chairs, opposite each other.* DAVID *doesn't look at* ANNA.

ANNA. . . . and so you see, and without wishing to belittle your your your . . . but it is essential that you understand just what we're dealing with, here. These traumatic confrontations with her past, combined with extreme clinical depression, have left her in the most fragile of mental states. A meeting such as this . . . well, I'm sure I don't have to labour the point, suffice to say that our priority must be to ensure that Lynn suffers no further damage as the result of your meeting.

Pause.

All of which means that, in order for your meeting to take place, there are certain, certain parameters that must be observed.

Pause.

Of course, I realise that you will have your own agenda, and that, in your circumstances, you may feel the need to apportion blame, and I would expect that, no doubt, the blame will be most easily directed towards me, but I would ask you, for the sake of communication, to place these feelings to one side, and to think of me as a kind of arbiter, as a a facilitator, who has, at heart, the same desire as yourself, which is, I'm sure, to see Lynn make a full and lasting recovery.

Pause.

Can we assume this as a base from which we might make a start?

Pause.

ANNA. Well, can we can we at least agree to try to behave as adults, and attempt a conversation.

Pause.

DAVID. You've never had kids, have you?

Pause.

ANNA. Kids?

DAVID. You've never had kids.

Pause.

ANNA. I don't understand the . . .

DAVID. It's just, you know, it just occurs to me that you can't know what it means. (*Pause.*) To have a child.

Pause.

ANNA. Well, just because . . .

DAVID. To create a a a . . .

ANNA. Just because I haven't . . .

DAVID. . . . you can't *know* what that's . . .

ANNA. . . . doesn't mean, doesn't mean I can't *appreciate* what . . .

DAVID. 'Appreciate'?

ANNA. . . . what it is, what it is to be a . . .

DAVID. You think you can 'appreciate' that?

ANNA. I think I can. Yes.

Pause.

DAVID. When Lynn was born, 'appreciate' this, when she was born, I was there. (*Pause.*) All through the labour, fourteen hours.

Pause.

ANNA. Let's not get ourselves side-tracked by . . .

DAVID. The head came out sideways, I expected to see a baby. All I saw? Eyes, deep blue eyes, wide open, no white, just blue, alien eyes, completely blue like the ocean.

ANNA. If we could . . .

DAVID. When they when they took her out, they counted fingers and toes, they wrapped her in a towel, they handed her to me, her head was covered in blood, red, glistening, I remember thinking, just for a second, that her brains were leaking. (*Pause.*) She closed her eyes, and cried, and she was mine, and I couldn't see anything else, and I kissed her on the head, I kissed her through the blood.

Pause.

Had it on my lips.

Pause.

They had to tell me to wipe it off. I'm wandering around the hospital, I've got blood on my lips.

Pause.

Can you 'appreciate' that?

Pause.

ANNA. You see, I don't believe it can serve any useful purpose for us to descend into pointless point-scoring . . .

DAVID. Pointless?

ANNA. My only concern is that you understand and accept the conditions of the meeting. Now, if you're prepared to listen, then we can make a start . . .

DAVID. I didn't come here to listen to . . .

ANNA. If you refuse . . .

DAVID. I was invited here . . .

ANNA. If you refuse to co-operate . . .

DAVID. . . . *by* Lynn . . .

ANNA. . . . . then Lynn has instructed me to ask you to leave.

Pause.

DAVID. She said that?

ANNA. She made herself quite . . .

DAVID. She 'instructed' you.

ANNA. That's right. Look, if we are to . . .

DAVID. Nothing to do with you?

Pause.

ANNA. Whatever Lynn chooses to do is . . .

DAVID. You just keep out of it?

ANNA. . . . her aff . . . Lynn is quite capable of making decisions for herself.

DAVID. Then let her come out here and tell me herself.

ANNA. No . . .

DAVID. Let her . . . *she* invited me, not you. *She* sent me the letter, she wants me to leave . . .

ANNA. The letter . . .

DAVID. . . . . she can tell me herself.

ANNA. The letter doesn't mean anything.

Pause.

DAVID. It doesn't . . . ?

ANNA. It doesn't mean what you think it means.

Pause.

DAVID. And what do I think it means?

Pause.

ANNA. I don't know, maybe, maybe she's changed her mind, had second thoughts, I realise it might look to you as if there's something to be *seen* . . .

DAVID. Lynn . . .

ANNA. . . . something in the *act* . . .

DAVID. *Lynn* sent *me* the . . .

ANNA. You mustn't make the mistake of thinking it might mean more than what it is, which is a simple . . .

DAVID. One second . . .

ANNA. . . . a simple invitation . . .

DAVID. If you would . . .

ANNA. . . . nothing more.

DAVID. If you would let me speak.

Pause.

I'm sure you're eminently qualified, and have any number of fascinating theories about me, but, to be frank, it's not your place to tell me what to think.

ANNA. Not my place?

DAVID. I'm not one of your 'patients'.

ANNA. And just what do you think 'my place' is?

Pause.

DAVID. I came here, at Lynn's invitation, and against the advice of my lawyer, to discuss this matter . . .

ANNA. There can be . . .

DAVID. . . . and I think you should . . .

ANNA. No, there can be no dis . . .

DAVID. I'd like you to go and get her now.

ANNA. There can be no 'discussion', you see? This is what I'm . . .

DAVID. I'd like to speak to my daughter.

Pause.

ANNA. There can be no meeting until you accept Lynn's conditions.

Pause.

DAVID. Lynn's conditions?

ANNA. That's right.

Pause.

DAVID. And what are these 'conditions'?

Pause.

ANNA. That you will listen to everything she has to say, without interruption. That you will accept all that she has remembered as fact, without . . .

DAVID. Fact?

ANNA. . . . without reservation. That you will acknowledge . . .

DAVID (*getting to his feet*). Wait, just . . .

ANNA. . . . acknowledge your . . .

DAVID. I acknowledge *nothing*. I accept *nothing*, you understand? What do you think, I came here like some some *child*, to be *told*, to be to be *accused*? I see no *facts*, there *are* no facts.

Pause.

ANNA. If you do not agree . . .

DAVID. I want to talk to my daughter.

ANNA. Not until . . .

DAVID. And if you don't go and get her now, I will.

Pause.

ANNA. You see, I really think you're . . .

DAVID. Did you hear what I . . . ?

ANNA. . . . I think you're deluding yourself, here.

DAVID (*calling offstage*). Lynn?

Pause.

ANNA. Because I think you believe that there's still a solution to all of this . . .

DAVID (*calling offstage*). Lynn?

ANNA. Do you know how sick your daughter is?

Pause.

That she's that she's close to suicidal?

Pause.

And you come here to talk about your*self*, make a case for your*self*, a martyr of your*self*, in the misguided hope that maybe you can garnish some sympathy, which would . . .

DAVID. No . . .

ANNA. . . . which would allow you to persuade her towards a solution that would make it easier for you.

DAVID. Easier?

ANNA. No. This is what I mean, you come here . . .

DAVID. You think this is easy for me?

ANNA. . . . you come with hope for for for, I don't know, as you said, discussion, maybe . . . some kind of reconciliation, perhaps . . . you must realise that none of these things will happen, here. (*Pause.*) But in so far as helping your daughter, to move forward into *healing*, you have a part to play, by listening, by accepting what she says as *fact*, by seeking her *forgiveness*, and so facilitating . . .

DAVID. Forgiveness?

ANNA. . . . perhaps, at Lynn's discretion, a way forward . . .

DAVID. You want me to ask for her forgiveness?

Pause.

ANNA. That's right.

DAVID. For what?

ANNA. You see?

DAVID. For what am I to be forgiven?

ANNA. This is what I'm trying to . . .

DAVID. Some dream?

ANNA. . . . I'm trying to explain . . .

DAVID. Some fantasy?

ANNA. You think you can come here . . .

DAVID. Some lunatic story you made up in the bath?

Pause.

Do you know what you've done to me? The past year? You have any idea what I've . . .

ANNA. Whatever might have happened to you . . .

DAVID. . . . my wife, my wife's in a bloody *hospital,* she can't bear to be *awake!*

Pause.

ANNA. This has no bearing on . . .

DAVID. Twenty years in a job, *twenty years*, they let me go, no hearing, nothing proved, no *facts*, I don't even get to *speak*, 'we'll have to let you go', I've had bricks through my windows, I've been stoned in the street, I drink, I get up in the morning, and I drink, and then I go to bed. That's all. That's me, that's all that's *left* me.

ANNA. Whatever you may have suffered . . .

DAVID. And you expect me to come here . . .

ANNA. . . . as a as a direct consequence of your own actions . . .

DAVID. . . . ask forgiveness for 'what I did', listen to 'what a bad *man* I am' . . .

ANNA. . . . it's nothing compared to what Lynn's been through, what she's going through. Don't you . . . you say you come to 'talk', I don't think you do.

DAVID. I know what I want, don't tell me what I . . .

ANNA. You want this all to be swept away, buried, forgotten . . .

DAVID. No . . .

ANNA. . . . you want to to to amputate your past, so you don't
have to confront what you did!

DAVID. How can I confront something that isn't there?

Pause.

ANNA. Well, of course, you would *say* that . . .

DAVID. I say it because it's true.

Pause.

ANNA. You're saying you have no memory of these events.

DAVID. I'm saying there are no events to remember. You think
I'd just forget something like this?

Pause.

ANNA. Whether you remember . . .

DAVID. . . . these 'claims' . . .

ANNA. Please listen . . .

DAVID. . . . these these these 'stories' . . .

ANNA. Whether you remember or not is irrelevant.

Pause.

DAVID. Irrelevant?

ANNA. All you have to understand is that *Lynn* believes . . .

DAVID. I *don't* understand, I don't even know where this *came*
from, all I know, all I know she meets you, she meets you,
and I'm this this monster I don't recognise, now you tell
me . . .

ANNA. The human memory is a complex . . .

DAVID. You . . . what about me, what about my memories,
don't they count?

ANNA. . . . it's a complex thing, we . . .

DAVID. You think I haven't tried? I don't sleep, I lie all I
    night, I relive every single moment since she was born, I *see
    everything*, and there's nothing there. There's *nothing there*.

Pause.

ANNA. Just because you claim not to remember . . .

DAVID. I *don't* remember.

ANNA. . . . it doesn't necessarily follow, you see, that these
    things did not happen.

Pause.

DAVID. How could they have happened, when I don't . . .

ANNA. There are many things we can't remember.

DAVID. No.

ANNA. Not through choice, we have no . . .

DAVID. I don't . . .

ANNA. Like maybe an accident, a traumatic event, we put
    them away, deny them, we bury them, repress them because
    they bring us pain.

DAVID. *No.* I don't . . . there would be something, some trace,
    some tiny *something* I'd remember.

ANNA. How can you know?

DAVID. I know, I remember, every moment, every . . .

ANNA. . . . how can you know for certain, you see?

DAVID. . . . every birthday, every Christmas . . .

ANNA. None of us can . . .

DAVID. . . . every gift I bought her, every expression on her
    face . . .

ANNA. No, we have no control over . . .

DAVID. My *own* childhood, before I could even walk, lying in
    my *pram*, for christ's sake . . .

ANNA. Please . . .

DAVID. . . . in a garden, I can still smell the *leaves*.

ANNA. It's not as simple as . . .

DAVID. When I was a kid, I remember my room, every *detail*,
it was a a small place, a peculiar shape, a sort of sort of *oval*
shape . . . no straight lines . . . the ceiling *curved* . . . the
carpet *brown* . . . with an oatmeal *fleck*, the walls were
painted *white*, but looked yellow in the lamplight.

ANNA. This is just . . .

DAVID. I used to lie in bed, *terrify* myself with car lights
sweeping the walls, like eyes inside the plaster, I can still
feel that panic.

ANNA. This proves nothing.

DAVID. My blankets, no, a question of memory, you said, so
you'll *listen* . . . my blankets were army surplus, they felt
fuzzy like an unshaven *chin*, used to itch your *skin*, I would
pull the top sheet up, and fold it over the blanket, so that it
protected me, and the sheet always felt stone cold on my
neck, I had one of those old reading lights, like a like a little
box, that clipped over the headboard, and had a little *cord*
with a *toggle*, which you *pulled* to switch it *on*, but it
flickered, and you had to *hit* it to get it to *work*, I had a
chest of *drawers*, with a matching *dressing* table, with an
arch shaped *mirror* that as far as I can remember, was
always *cracked*, the *crack* went across the top left hand *side*,
looked like a piece of *paper* with a folded *corner*.

Pause.

ANNA. We can all of us . . .

DAVID. My *bed* . . . small, not comfy, lumpy mattress, old,
stained from when I used to *wet* it when I was younger, I
remember one night wakening up, I got to my knees, still
half asleep, I remember looking down, I can *see* the stream,
like an slow arc through the air, I can *hear* the sound it
made as it landed on the sheets, like water shooting from
the overflow pipe, landing on concrete outside the house.

Pause.

One of the drawers always *stuck*, there was a knack to *opening* it, you had to do it at a slight *angle*, if it was here, now, I would still be able to *open* that drawer . . . each drawer had two *knobs*, half a globe of imitation brass, half a globe of black *plastic*, I discovered at an early *age*, that you could un*screw* the knobs, the top half of the globe would come *away*, and inside you could see the *screw*, I could sit for *hours*, dragging my *thumb*nail along the *screw* . . .

ANNA. I don't know what you think you're . . .

DAVID. . . . which made, which made a Completely. Fucking. Satisfying *ratchet* noise, a noise that would start low in *pitch*, then rise *higher* the nearer my finger came to the *front*, I always imagined it sounded like a *trumpet*, and I'd try to play *tunes* on it, which sounded fine to *me*, but used to irritate the *fuck* out everyone else.

Pause.

The bottom drawer of the *chest* was where I kept my *drawings* and *poems* and, when I was a little older, stupid adolescent *stories* about *shagging* and people generally *dying*.

Pause.

The second drawer up housed *T- Shirts*, or Slippy Fucking *Joes*, as my mother called them, which were invariably Fucking Woolworths, with a Completely. Wonderful. Fucking. Ladybird on the *label*, the third drawer up contained *jumpers*, mostly *hand knitted* by my mum, alien shaped lumps of *dead fucking sheep*, with *tight fucking necks* that used to *catch* your fucking *nose*, and *mince* your fucking *face* when you tried to take them *off*, and my mum used to get *angry* if I pulled them off by the *neck*, because, she claimed, it *stretched* them and put them put them out of fucking *shape*, but I could never master the crossed-arms-lift-from-the-bottom, which took the jumper off inside *out*, which seemed just *plain fucking stupid* to me, and, anyway, I could never understand why she wanted to *preserve* that fucking shape in the *first* place, if you looked into a mirror wearing one of the jumpers, you were always convinced the sheep was in there *with* you.

Pause.

The *fourth drawer up* contained fucking *underwear*, the *top fucking drawer*, fucking *socks*, mainly fucking *ankle*, favourite pair – gold and black fucking *hoops* cos they fucking *looked* like fucking *wasps*.

Pause.

I was five years old.

Pause.

That's thirty five years ago.

Long pause.

ANNA. And what do you think this proves?

Pause.

DAVID. That I remember, that my memory is clear.

ANNA. And so you'll tell her she's wrong, and you're right, what do you think that will achieve? As far as Lynn's concerned, *she's* in the right, she's convinced, you've already *lost* her, *our* job . . .

DAVID. I want her to tell me that.

ANNA. Our job . . .

DAVID. I want to hear her say it.

ANNA. You'll only make it worse for her. Don't you see that? What do you think you can make her change her mind? You can you can *persuade* her with a a a hug and a few choice words? She *believes*. Nothing you can say can make any difference to that belief, even if she was wrong, it wouldn't matter.

DAVID. Of course it . . .

ANNA. No. Nothing matters. Nothing matters but Lynn, and how we can help her to heal. Surely you must agree with that.

Pause.

DAVID. I . . . I can talk to her, if I can just . . .

ANNA. If you have her interests at heart . . .

DAVID. Wait a second . . .

ANNA. . . . . then then surely you want to put yourself to one side, do what's best for *her*, what helps *her*.

Pause.

Isn't that what you want?

Pause.

DAVID. You're turning . . .

ANNA. Don't you want to see your daughter get better?

Pause.

DAVID. You *say* that, you *say* she's . . . you *say* she's sick, how do I know? I haven't even seen her, I'm meant to trust *you*, believe what you . . .

ANNA. What do you want, a second opinion? There's no time, don't you understand? She's sick *now,* she needs help *now.* Why do you think she asked you to come?

Pause.

DAVID. I don't under . . .

ANNA. She invited you here, because she needs your help.

Pause.

Of course, she doesn't see it that way, she thinks she's brought you here to confront you, but I know, I've been watching her, every day, grow smaller and smaller under the weight of all this.

Pause.

DAVID. So, what're you saying, I don't see . . .

ANNA. I'm saying you can make a difference, here. I'm saying that regardless of what's happened between you,

who's right or wrong, you have a chance to repair the
damage, to bridge the gulf between you. I'm saying she
needs you, she needs you now.

DAVID. She *needs* me?

ANNA. More than she ever did.

DAVID. She's the one *accusing* me!

Pause.

ANNA. And is that all you can see? Accusations, your
'reputation', is that all she means to you?

Pause.

DAVID. I . . . I don't . . .

Pause.

ANNA. She's your daughter. If you love her, you'll do
everything in your power to let her live, you won't question
her belief.

Pause.

DAVID. Wait a minute . . .

ANNA. That could do her more damage than . . .

DAVID. Wait a minute, wait . . . you want me to *admit* to this?

Pause.

ANNA. If you love your daughter . . .

DAVID. You want me to admit to something never even
happened?

ANNA. How much do you love her?

Pause.

DAVID. I don't believe this.

ANNA. Do you care if she lives or dies?

DAVID. I don't believe . . . you're asking me to . . .

ANNA. You say that you love her.

DAVID. Of course I . . .

ANNA. Then prove it.

Pause.

DAVID. You want me to *confess* to being this *monster*?

ANNA. I want you to save your daughter's life!

Pause. Enter LYNN, carrying some sheets of paper. DAVID turns to see her. They stare at each other for a moment.

LYNN crosses to one of the chairs.

DAVID. It's so good to see you.

Pause.

LYNN. I'd like to read you something, and I'd like to get through it without interruption.

Pause.

DAVID. How are you?

LYNN. What?

Pause.

DAVID. How . . . how have you been?

Pause. LYNN consults her list.

LYNN. The following is a list of memories, recovered through hypnosis over the past year and a half. These memories concern sexual abuse at your hands, and have been suppressed for most of my life. A full copy of this statement has been formally lodged with the police. (*Pause.*) My reasons for reading this to you include a demand that you acknowledge your responsibility, and a need to redefine our relationship, in that I no longer consider us to be father and daughter, that is to say, I hereby disown you as my father.

DAVID. Lynn . . .

LYNN. I'll read the list now.

DAVID. Lynn, listen to me . . .

LYNN. No! I'm not interested in anything you have to say, and if . . .

DAVID. Please . . .

LYNN. . . . *if* you persist in interrupting, then I'll leave.

Pause.

DAVID. I only want to tell you that I love you.

Pause.

And that, despite all of this . . .

LYNN. *Do you want me to leave?*

Pause.

DAVID. No.

LYNN. Then do me the courtesy of listening.

DAVID. I have to tell you something.

LYNN. No . . .

DAVID. Whatever you remember . . .

LYNN. I want you to listen, I want you to *hear* this!

DAVID. If we could just talk. Please.

Pause.

LYNN (*reading from her list*). My earliest memories revolve around bathtime. I was about three when you started taking me into the bath with you. Being an inquisitive child, I was fascinated by the fact that you had a penis, and I didn't. You'd encourage me to touch it, and this grew into a game we'd play, like hide and seek, where I had to hunt for your penis under the water.

DAVID. Lynn . . .

LYNN. Of course, I was too young to realise the significance of your erection, or that there was anything abnormal in your ejaculations.

DAVID. God, no.

LYNN. I'd find it funny, to the extent that I'd look forward to it, and then it would all be washed away. The game abruptly stopped when I mentioned it to my mother, but you dismissed it all as my fertile imagination, and of course, she believed you.

DAVID. This is just . . .

LYNN. *You'll listen to this, goddamn you!* This was *my* life, *my childhood*, and you took it away, you took it away, everything I *was*, everything I could have *been*, you rubbed it out.

DAVID. If you would just listen to me . . .

LYNN. There's nothing you can *say*, do you understand? There's nothing . . .

DAVID. Whatever you remember . . .

LYNN. No!

DAVID. Whatever I'm supposed to have done . . .

LYNN (*to* ANNA). You were right.

LYNN *gets to her feet.*

I was wrong to invite you.

DAVID. Wait.

LYNN *heads for the exit.* DAVID *stands in her way.*

DAVID. Lynn!

LYNN. Get out of my way.

DAVID. Listen . . .

LYNN. No.

She tries to pass him, he reaches out to her.

DAVID. You have to . . .

LYNN (*backing away, terrified*). Don't touch me!

ANNA *gets to her feet, goes to stand between* LYNN *and* DAVID.

DAVID. I only want to . . .

LYNN. Don't let him touch me!

DAVID. Lynn?

ANNA. It's okay.

LYNN. Don't let him . . .

ANNA. He won't touch you, he won't.

Pause.

(*To* DAVID.) Please . . .

DAVID steps back.

DAVID. I didn't mean to . . .

ANNA. It's okay.

DAVID. I only wanted to . . .

ANNA (*to* DAVID). Are we finished here? (*Pause. To* LYNN.) Come on.

She tries to put her arm around LYNN, *who holds up her hands to stop her.*

LYNN. I'm okay.

LYNN heads for the exit. ANNA *turns to* DAVID.

ANNA. You have nothing to say?

DAVID watches LYNN *until she's almost through the exit.*

DAVID. Okay, I won't deny it!

LYNN stops, turns. Pause.

LYNN. What did you say?

Pause.

DAVID. I'll . . . whatever you want, just . . .

LYNN. What did you just say?

Pause.

DAVID. I'm saying, I don't want to lose you, Lynn.

Pause.

LYNN. I don't understand.

DAVID. I'm prepared to do whatever it takes to help you.

LYNN. Help me?

She looks at ANNA.

What is this?

Pause.

Anna?

ANNA. Listen to him.

LYNN. What's happened here?

ANNA. Listen to what he has to say.

LYNN. What does he mean 'help me'? I don't need his help.

ANNA. Just give him a few . . .

LYNN. No! I don't need his . . . I need his confession, I want to hear him admit it.

DAVID. Lynn, please . . .

LYNN. What are you saying, are you saying you admit to these things?

Pause.

DAVID. . . . what . . . whatever you remember, and and you must realise that I have no memory of . . . but, I'm willing to . . .

LYNN. Do you admit it?

DAVID. . . . I'm willing to . . . concede the possibility that I might have . . .

LYNN. Possibility? These are not 'possibilities', these are facts.

DAVID. Whatever . . .

LYNN. No . . .

DAVID. Maybe we can . . . we can work together to . . .

LYNN. No, these are the facts, this is the truth, and I want you to admit it.

Pause.

DAVID. I . . .

LYNN (*resuming reading*). These incidents continued for several years . . .

DAVID. Wait . . .

ANNA. Let him speak, Lynn . . .

LYNN. . . . always in the form of games, always centred upon getting me to touch you.   ·

ANNA. Lynn . . .

LYNN. No, Anna . . .

DAVID. If we could just . . .

LYNN. My next vivid memory occurred when I was six. My mother was gone for the weekend, and one night I woke up to find your penis in my mouth. I couldn't breath, you kept forcing it to the back of my throat . . .

DAVID. No!

LYNN. I was gagging, struggling for air. You were calling me names, horrible names, 'you little fuck, you little cunt' . . .

DAVID. No!

LYNN. . . . my head was throbbing, I didn't understand, I was so confused. You came in my mouth, and you left.

DAVID. How can you say this, how can you . . .

LYNN. I threw up on the floor.

DAVID. Lynn?

LYNN. In the morning, you told me I'd had a bad dream, and made me clean up the vomit. But you were so nice to me, so understanding, I believed it was a dream. Until it happened again that night, when I decided to bite down hard on your penis, I had blood in my mouth, and you screamed, and you went into the garden, and came back with a stick, which you used to beat me with until I was sick from crying too much.

DAVID. Please stop this.

LYNN (*raising her voice*). You told me, you told me that if I ever mentioned it to anyone, I would die.

DAVID. Please . . .

LYNN. You said you'd placed a bomb inside my head, that was set to go off the minute I said anything about the abuse. You said you'd done this because I didn't love you. When I told you that I did, you said I had to prove it, by keeping quiet, by doing everything you told me. I grew up believing that everything was my fault, that I was being punished because I didn't love you. I'd try to prove I did, I'd give you hugs and kisses, and then I'd be rewarded, you'd buy me something nice. But you'd wait until I did something wrong, and then you'd abuse me again, until I came to associate the abuse with being bad. Which meant, of course, that it was all my fault again. One time, we went on a day out, we took a picnic. You bought me a new dress, I remember it had tiny little flowers. You took me into some woods, found a quiet spot away from everyone and everything, then you raped me, both vaginal and anal rape.

DAVID. Enough!

LYNN. I haven't finished.

DAVID. I won't hear anymore!

LYNN. Because it's the truth?

DAVID. No.

LYNN. You said you wouldn't deny it.

DAVID. No, that was, that was . . .

LYNN (*resuming reading*). I was in agony for weeks.

DAVID. I thought you were . . .

LYNN. My mother wanted to take me to a doctor, but you talked her out of it.

DAVID. She told me, listen to me, she told me . . .

LYNN. She asked me what happened that day, and I couldn't tell her, because I didn't want the bomb to go off. But she had her suspicions, and tried to confront you. Again, you managed to talk your way out of it, by blaming me. But from then on, things got much worse for me. I made the first attempt to kill myself. I thought of drowning myself in the bath, but I couldn't face that. So I stabbed myself in my belly with a knife . . .

DAVID. That's not how it . . .

LYNN. . . . I have the scar to prove it.

DAVID. But that's not how it happened, Lynn. It was an accident, remember?

LYNN. An accident?

DAVID. You you you fell . . .

LYNN. I fell.

DAVID. . . . you fell on the knife.

LYNN. How could I . . .

DAVID. Don't you remember?

LYNN. How could I fall on a knife?

Pause.

DAVID. No, you must remember . . .

LYNN. How could that happen?

DAVID. . . . in the kitchen, you fell on the floor.

LYNN. How could I fall on a knife? What, was it sticking up?

DAVID. It was an accident.

LYNN. Sticking up in the air?

DAVID. You're getting . . .

LYNN. Sitting on the floor, waiting for someone to fall on it?

Pause.

LYNN (*continuing to read*). The hospital recommended I undergo psychological treatment, but of course, you could never allow that. Instead, we moved to the city, this city. And then, I began to grow smarter, or so I thought. I realised that my body was worth something to you. I would use this to get things – at first, toys, but later it was cigarettes, dresses, records, make-up. You used to to tell me how to make myself up. I consoled myself by pretending I was making you pay. Meanwhile, my mother grew more withdrawn – she had a rough idea by now what was going on, but she slipped so easily into denial, I couldn't talk to her. She'd say that you spoiled me, she started drinking, anything to avoid the truth. It was about this time that you first introduced me to one of your friends.

During the following, ANNA *turns nauseous, is forced to take a seat.*

You took me to a hotel, and hired a room. In the room, you produced a rope, and tied me to the bed.

DAVID. No.

LYNN. You then beat me, and warned me to co-operate, or the next beating could kill me.

DAVID. No!

LYNN. Your friend . . . I can't remember his name yet . . . he came in and had sex with me, anally.

DAVID. This isn't true, none of this is . . .

LYNN. He came in my hair.

DAVID. No!

LYNN. All I could do was lie there and think of how much this was going to cost you.

DAVID (*going for* ANNA). You fucking bitch!

LYNN *stands in his way.*

LYNN. Don't touch her!

DAVID. I'll fucking kill her!

LYNN. Oh, that's right, that's what you do, isn't it.

DAVID. I'll fucking . . .

LYNN. Beat us up, go on. Get it done. I took it before, I can take it now!

DAVID suddenly goes berserk. He upends all the boxes in a blind rage, spilling the contents all over the stage, during the following . . .

DAVID. You'll fucking listen! You'll fucking listen to me!

LYNN. Stop it!

DAVID. You'll fucking . . . none of this is me!

LYNN. Stop this now!

DAVID. None of it! Not me! Not me!

Pause. He runs out of steam, ends up on the floor amongst the mess.

Not me.

Pause.

Not me.

Long pause. DAVID *eventually looks around the mess.*

DAVID. I . . .

Pause.

All I want . . .

Pause. DAVID's *eyes fall on the photograph of himself with* LYNN. *He picks it up, stares at it.*

You kept this?

Pause.

You . . .

DAVID *has an almighty struggle to fight back a sudden surge of tears.*

Pause.

If we . . .

Pause.

If we could just leave ourselves behind.

Pause.

Just . . . *start.*

Pause.

Nothing counted, nothing judged, nothing . . . *known.*

Pause.

DAVID. Oh Lynn, I know I was never the best of fathers. That that I was selfish, maybe, sometimes, sometimes even cruel. (*Pause.*) But I loved you. (*Pause.*) I still do.

ANNA (*almost to herself*). He's lying.

DAVID. If we can only find somewhere . . .

ANNA. I know he's lying.

DAVID. . . . somewhere to start . . .

ANNA. . . . always lying, always telling you they love you, making you believe them . . .

LYNN. Anna?

ANNA. . . . your only chance is not to hear them, never listen, block out their words, never *see* them . . .

LYNN. Anna?

Pause.

ANNA (*surprised by the words*). . . . never love them.

Pause.

DAVID. Lynn, please, listen, hear me . . .

LYNN. I can't . . .

DAVID. This is her, all of this, it's her, Lynn.

LYNN. I . . .

DAVID. She's she's . . . I don't know what it is she's done, but we can get beyond that, we can . . .

LYNN. No! This is *you!* I *see* it, I *remember*.

DAVID. . . . we can find something . . .

LYNN. You did these things to me.

DAVID. If you would only . . .

LYNN. You said you wouldn't deny it.

DAVID. That was her too, don't you see?

LYNN. What?

DAVID. She told me, she told me I had to confess.

Pause.

LYNN. Anna?

Pause.

DAVID. That I had to confess, or you'd kill yourself.

Pause.

LYNN. You told him that?

DAVID. Now do you see? This is what she *does*, Lynn.

Pause.

LYNN. Anna?

Pause.

ANNA. I . . .

LYNN. Did you say that?

Pause.

ANNA. I think we should . . . I don't feel . . .

LYNN. Did you ask him to confess?

Pause.

ANNA. I don't . . .

LYNN. Did you . . .

ANNA (*still distant*). He's . . . he's . . . I had to protect you from . . .

LYNN (*to* ANNA). I told you not to . . .

ANNA. . . . from his his his lying and his twisting . . .

LYNN. I told you . . .

ANNA. This is what I tried to *tell* you!

Pause.

LYNN. I don't *believe* you could . . . I told you not to interfere, Anna.

Pause.

That this was *my thing*, that it had to come from *me!*

Pause.

LYNN. And now you've *ruined* it for me.

ANNA. No . . .

LYNN. How could you?

ANNA. I . . .

LYNN. How could you do this to me?

ANNA. Don't you see it? (*Pause.*) Don't you see what I see?

Pause.

You think he, you think he cares, about you, about anything but what he can *get* from you?

Pause.

LYNN. I . . . I can't . . .

ANNA. You know what he is.

LYNN. I can't *think*, I can't . . .

ANNA. You've *seen* what he is!

Pause.

DAVID (*to* ANNA). Who the fuck do you think you are?

Pause.

That you can treat us like this.

ANNA. See it, Lynn!

DAVID (*getting to his feet*). Just tell me, you tell me, who the fuck *are* you? My daughter, *my* daughter, she moves *in* with you . . . we don't even know who the fuck you are? (*To* LYNN.) What are you doing, Lynn? Living with . . . with *this*.

Pause.

DAVID (*to* ANNA). Tell me, just . . . what gives you the *right* to *decide* for *me*, for *Lynn*, who she *sees*, who she *doesn't*, what she *thinks*, about *me*, about *anything*, twenty years my *life*, were you there? *Were you there?* I don't *recognise* you, you understand?

ANNA. Watch him, Lynn, are you watching?

DAVID. I don't *accept* you.

ANNA. Take a look at what he is.

DAVID. I'm her father! What are you? Somebody she *met*?

ANNA. That's right.

DAVID. Somebody she *picked up*?

ANNA. Go on.

DAVID. Some fucked up lonely old *cunt*, thinks she can walk right in . . .

LYNN. That's enough!

DAVID. . . . fuck with people's *lives*, d'you get some kind of *kick* from that?

ANNA (*to* LYNN). What did I tell you?

DAVID. Is that it? Your your your *perversion*? You get *off* on this?

LYNN. I said that's enough.

DAVID. No. It's not enough, it's not nearly enough. (*To* ANNA.) Just tell me, what do you get from this . . . this arrangement? As far as I remember, Lynn has no money, so what do you get? What's your 'fee'?

ANNA (*to* LYNN). Didn't I tell you? That it would come to this?

DAVID (*to* LYNN). Where do you sleep, Lynn?

LYNN. What?

DAVID. Where do you sleep? Or hasn't she got round to that, yet?

Pause.

LYNN. Get out!

DAVID. She will.

LYNN. I'm calling the police.

DAVID. Go ahead. (*Pause.*) Go on, bring them here, because I'm going to tell you something, I don't care anymore. And that's the truth. I've spent the last year of my life grasping every fucking straw, I've had enough. (*To* ANNA.) You you talk about me, about 'what I am', well let me tell you, I know *you*, lady, I know what *you* are.

LYNN. Get out of this house!

DAVID. And I know what goes on in that sick mind of yours.

Pause.

DAVID *suddenly grabs* LYNN's *list from her hand.*

LYNN. What're you . . .

DAVID. This!

LYNN. Give me that.

DAVID (*to* ANNA). This is you, right?

LYNN. Give me it!

DAVID (*to* ANNA). This sick fucking mess, this is your head, right? That's what all this is about . . .

LYNN. I said, give it to me!

DAVID (*looking at the list*). . . . he came in my mouth . . . (*He gets closer to* ANNA, *she stands her ground.*) . . . vaginal, anal rape . . . (*And closer still.*) . . . tied me to the bed . . . that's what this is . . .

ANNA (*afraid*). You don't scare me.

DAVID. This is what goes on in your fucking *head*, this is your *guilt*, here!

ANNA. I won't be afraid of you.

DAVID. Your your sick fucking fantasies, and you can't live with them, you can't live with the guilt of *thinking* them!

ANNA. I won't . . .

DAVID. You know why?

ANNA. I won't . . .

DAVID. . . . because they *turn you on.*

Pause. LYNN *tries to pull* DAVID *away.*

LYNN. Get away from her!

ANNA. It's okay.

LYNN. Get . . .

ANNA. I'm not afraid.

DAVID. Much easier if it really happened, much easier if there's someone to *blame!*

LYNN. Get away from her!

ANNA *continues to stand her ground, but she's beginning to panic.*

DAVID (*inches from* ANNA). . . . beat me with a stick . . . how can you *live* with this? . . . had sex with me anally . . .

ANNA. I won't be afraid.

DAVID (*right up to her face*). . . . he came in my hair! This is you, right? This is what you want!

DAVID *grabs her by the hair, yanks back her head, holds the list to her nose.*

LYNN. No!

DAVID. Look at it! Take a look! Do you see yourself?

LYNN. Leave her!

DAVID. Do you see yourself?

LYNN. Fucking leave her!

DAVID. You disgust me!

DAVID *pushes* ANNA *away.* ANNA *falls to the floor.*

LYNN. Anna.

LYNN *rushes to help her, but* ANNA *struggles, tries to get away.*

ANNA. Don't touch me!

LYNN. Anna.

ANNA. Don't let him touch me!

LYNN. Anna?

ANNA. I don't want . . . I don't want him to . . . *don't let him touch me!*

LYNN. Anna, it's me.

ANNA. Oh my God, oh my God . . .

LYNN. What is it?

ANNA. I can't . . .

LYNN. What is it, what's wrong?

ANNA. I can't breath.

LYNN. Take it easy.

ANNA. I can't . . . I can't get my . . .

LYNN. Take it easy, now.

ANNA. Oh my God.

LYNN. Easy.

ANNA. I can't . . .

LYNN. Deep breaths . . .

ANNA. I can't . . .

LYNN. Slowly, nice and slow . . .

ANNA. I can see . . .

LYNN. Nice and slow . . .

ANNA. It's him.

LYNN. What?

Pause.

ANNA. I can see.

LYNN. What? What can you see?

Pause.

ANNA. No, this can't . . .

LYNN. Anna?

ANNA. This can't be, this can't . . .

LYNN. What is it?

ANNA. I can see him.

LYNN. Who? Who can you see?

Pause.

ANNA. The hotel, I can . . .

LYNN. What?

ANNA. The hotel . . . the hotel room, how can this . . .

LYNN. The hotel? What hotel?

ANNA. I can see him, I can smell him.

LYNN. Who?

ANNA. No.

LYNN. Who do you see, Anna?

ANNA. No!

LYNN. Who do you see?

Pause.

ANNA. My . . .

Pause.

LYNN. Your..?

ANNA. I saw my f . . .

Long pause.

LYNN. Your father?

ANNA. He came in the room.

LYNN. I don't understand.

ANNA. He came in the room with his friends, I don't . . .

LYNN. I don't understand . . . you . . . you said the hotel.

ANNA. Can't move, can't breathe.

LYNN. I don't . . .

ANNA. The pain, so much pain, in my arms, in my body . . .

Pause.

LYNN. No, this is . . . this is . . . it's my memory, Anna,
   you're . . . you're reliving . . .

ANNA. Four of them.

Pause.

There were four of them.

Pause.

Oh my God, I remember!

LYNN. No . . .

ANNA. I remember!

Long pause. ANNA *seems to come round, looks at* LYNN.

Oh Lynn.

LYNN. It's okay.

ANNA. What have I done?

LYNN. It's okay.

ANNA. What have I . . .

Pause.

I'm so sorry.

LYNN. It's okay.

ANNA. I remember, Lynn.

LYNN. You're just . . .

ANNA. I see him.

LYNN. Just let it go.

ANNA. I see him!

LYNN. Let it go.

Pause.

ANNA. I'm so so sorry.

Pause.

DAVID. No way.

LYNN *turns to looks at* DAVID.

LYNN. What have you done to her?

DAVID. No fucking . . . what have *I* done? You mean you believe this this this . . .

LYNN. How could you . . .

DAVID. It's garbage, Lynn, all of this, it's just . . .

LYNN. No.

DAVID. . . . she's she's a fake Lynn, she's doing this to get you to . . .

LYNN. No!

DAVID. . . . to get your sympathy, because she *knows*, she . . .

LYNN. She remembered.

DAVID. Come on . . .

LYNN. You saw her.

DAVID. . . . you can't be taken in by . . .

LYNN. She remembered. Like I did.

DAVID. Open your eyes, Lynn.

LYNN. It's all so clear to me now.

DAVID. She's making this . . .

LYNN. Before, it was just flashes, dreams . . . now I can feel it.

DAVID. She's she's . . .

LYNN. Now, it's real.

DAVID. It's all garbage, Lynn.

LYNN. Watching you treat her like you treated me . . .

DAVID. You can't . . .

LYNN. Like she was nothing to you!

DAVID. I had to . . .

LYNN. Like she was filth!

DAVID. I had to *show* you . . .

LYNN. And I felt it. I felt your hands on *me*, how you treated *me*, all those *years* . . .

DAVID. No, this whole . . . these memories, they're all . . .

LYNN. I don't care about the memories, I don't *need* the memories to know what you are, to know what you think of me.

Pause.

DAVID. I love you, you *know* that.

LYNN. How can you say that when you treat us like you do?

Pause.

DAVID. I . . . I had to . . .

LYNN. I *felt* it, don't you see?

Pause.

DAVID. I . . .

LYNN. Whatever you do to her, you do to me.

Pause.

DAVID. I don't understand, I only . . .

LYNN. No, you don't understand, you don't understand what it is to endure so much hate, so much disgust, but by God, you will, from now on, you will, because that's what I feel for you. That's what you've given me, that's all you've ever given me, and I don't want to be feeling this . . .

DAVID. I . . .

LYNN. . . . but for as long as I'm breathing, that's all you'll ever get from me.

Pause.

DAVID. Lynn . . .

LYNN. Get out!

Pause.

There's nothing left for you here.

LYNN *goes back to help* ANNA. DAVID*'s eyes fall on the photograph of himself with* LYNN. *He picks it up.*

DAVID. You kept this.

Pause.

Lynn?

Pause. LYNN *turns back.*

You you you kept this, that must mean . . .

LYNN. Do you recognise it?

Pause.

DAVID. I . . .

LYNN. Do you know when it was taken?

Pause.

DAVID. It doesn't matter, you kept it, you see, that's . . .

LYNN. It was the day of picnic.

Pause.

DAVID. The day of the picnic . . .

LYNN. The day you raped me.

Long pause. DAVID *holds out the photograph to* LYNN.

DAVID. Then I don't remember it.

Pause. LYNN *makes no move to take the photograph.*

LYNN. And I don't need it anymore.

Pause. DAVID *continues to hold out the photograph for a moment, as he looks at* LYNN. *He opens his fingers, lets the photograph fall to the floor.*

DAVID *exits.* LYNN *turns to* ANNA.

LYNN. You okay?

ANNA. I never knew . . .

LYNN. It's okay.

ANNA. I never . . . I'm so sorry.

LYNN. Don't blame yourself.

ANNA. I had no idea, you must believe that.

LYNN. I do.

ANNA. But your memories . . .

LYNN. They still belong to me.

ANNA. But how can they . . .

LYNN. Ssh.

ANNA. I saw him in the hotel.

LYNN. Ssh.

ANNA. I saw him.

LYNN. Easy now.

   LYNN *hugs* ANNA, *kisses her on the top of the head.*

ANNA. . . . how can we know . . .

LYNN. Ssh.

   Pause.

ANNA. . . . what's yours, what's mine..?

LYNN. We'll start again. (*Pause.*) We'll unpick it.

   Pause.

   Like you said.

   Pause.

   The new frontier.

   End of play.

A Nick Hern Book

Anna Weiss first published in Great Britain in 1997
as a paperback original by Nick Hern Books Limited,
14 Larden Road, London W3 7ST, in association with
the Traverse Theatre, Edinburgh

Front cover photo by Euan Myles

Typeset by Country Setting, Woodchurch, Kent, TN26 3TB

Printed and bound in Great Britain by Cox and Wyman Ltd,
Reading, Berks

ISBN 1 85459 388 9

A CIP catalogue record for this book is available from
the British Library